Clay Characters 101

Create 20

whimsical figures

with polymer clay

Becky Meverden

Published by

krause publications
An F&W Publications Company
700 East State Street • Iola, WI 54990-0001
715-445-2214 • 888-457-2873
www.krause.com

Please call or write for our free catalog of publications. Our toll-free number to place an order or obtain a free catalog is 800-258-0929, or please use our regular business telephone 715-445-2214.

Step-by-step photography by Curt Meverden.
All projects by Becky Meverden.

ISBN: 0-87349-523-3

Dedication

To my family—Curt, Laura, Luke, Mom and Dad, Wendy and Heidi, and my in-laws, Chuck and Alice, for always supporting me no matter what.

Acknowledgments

To my husband, Curt, for taking the step-by-step photographs for this book. I could not have done this without you. You are my rock.

To Maureen Carlson, thank you for your support and friendship. You are an amazing talent.

To Carol Duvall of HGTV's *The Carol Duvall Show,* thank you for graciously sharing me with your viewers. You truly are "The Queen of Crafts."

To Holly Hughes, my first producer on *The Carol Duvall Show,* thank you for all your insight and patience.

I would also like to thank Polyform Products for supplying all the polymer clay used in the projects.

Table of Contents

Introduction 4

The Basics 5
Types of Polymer Clay 5
Tips 6
Conditioning the Clay 6
Basic Tools 6
Basic Shapes 8

Projects 9
Candy Cane Log 10
Babies and Blanket 11
Chocolate Kiss Guy 14
Clown 16
Firefighter 19
Ladybug and Clay Pot 22
Snail and Friend Eraser 24
Wacky Bird 26

Pen Projects 28
How to Cover a Pen with
Polymer Clay 29
Humpty Dumpty Pen 30
Jester Pen 32
Sea Life Pen 34

Holiday Projects 36
Sweet Heart 37
Bunny and Chick Easter Eggs 39
Halloween Pumpkin Cat and Ghost 42
Thanksgiving Couple 44
Ginger and Fred Christmas Ornaments 47

Resources 48

Introduction

Polymer clay was introduced to me in 1991 by a neighbor who made polymer clay miniatures. The adorable figurines seemed so complicated to a novice like me, but when she broke it down into a few simple shapes, I was hooked. I will never forget my first sale at a craft show and the many smiles I received from shoppers as they approached my booth.

There are no rules in the world of polymer clay. Discover for yourself how fun and satisfying this medium is. The characters in this book will bring a smile to your face. The only prerequisites are a desire to learn and an adventurous spirit. Use this book as a tool that will give you the skills to begin your journey. Watch as balls of clay come to life as little characters. They seem to take on personalities all their own. But I should warn you. Polymer clay is addictive. It is hard to put it down.

So now amaze your friends and family. Let the journey begin and see where it takes you.

The Basics

Types of Polymer Clay

There are many different polymer clays to choose from. I have worked with all of them and found they all have strengths and weaknesses. It usually comes down to which clay would work best for the specific project I'm working on. Following are short descriptions of the polymer clays available to date.

Eraser Clay—Manufactured by Polyform Products. It comes in six bright colors plus brown and white. This clay is very easy to condition. It becomes a pencil eraser after it is baked.

Fimo Classic—Manufactured by Eberhard Faber. It is the most difficult of the clays to condition. It helps to use a softener such as MixQuick to soften it. It is a great clay for caning and is very strong after baking.

Fimo Soft—Manufactured by Eberhard Faber. It is easily conditioned and strong after baking. It is much easier to work with than Fimo Classic.

Granitex—Manufactured by Polyform Products. It is called the "stone-like" clay and is easy to condition. The clay contains tiny fibers, which makes it not a good choice for caning. It comes in pastel colors.

Kato Polyclay—Developed by Donna Kato and Van Aken International. It is easy to condition and also a very strong clay. It is great for caning.

Premo! Sculpey—Manufactured by Polyform Products. It is easy to condition and very strong after baking. Premo! Sculpey was used in all the projects in this book with the exception of the Snail and Friend Eraser.

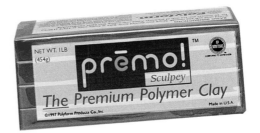

Sculpey III—Manufactured by Polyform Products. It is a great clay for beginners and for children. It is very soft and conditions very quickly. It is more brittle after baking than the other clays.

Tips

• A clean work surface is very important. Polymer clay can pick up dust, lint, and fibers. I use a piece of glass that I had made at my local glass store. You can use a variety of surfaces: countertop, ceramic tile, index card, or poster board. Don't use a surface that will also be used for food.

• Your hands need to be clean before you start. I use a waterless hand cleaner, and I dry my hands on paper towels. You also need to clean your hands between colors. Red really stains your hands, and if you switch to white without washing your hands, your white will turn into pink.

• The projects can be completed with, at the most, one 2 oz. block of each color listed under materials. If more than one block is needed, it will be stated. Some of the projects require mixing of colors. Take both balls of clay and roll them together into logs again and again until the colors are mixed with no lines of each individual color showing.

Conditioning the Clay

The polymer clay needs to be conditioned before you begin. Cut the clay into pieces and begin to roll it into a log. Keep twisting and rolling the clay until it no longer cracks and is warm. It should be soft and pliable. I have had pieces crack after baking because I didn't condition the clay properly.

Basic Tools

The wide range of tools that you can use with polymer clay is amazing. I started simply with a paring knife and round toothpicks. One of my favorite tools is a paintbrush. Not the brush end, but the blunt end. It is great for indenting. Tools that are used for polymer clay should never be used for food.

Cutting tools—Tissue blades and paring knives are great to cut polymer clay. Wallpaper blades also work well.

Needle tools—Round toothpicks, large sewing needles, or a ball stylus can be used to make the squint lines in the eyes of the figurines.

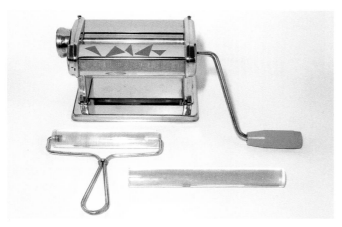

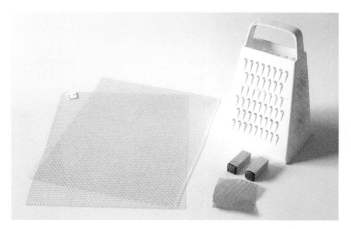

Rollers—Pasta makers, acrylic brayers, and acrylic rollers are used to flatten the polymer clay. A clay-dedicated rolling pin can also be used.

Pasta Maker Settings

Setting	#1	#2	#3	#4	#5
Inches	⅛"	⁷⁄₆₄"	³⁄₃₂"	⁵⁄₆₄"	¹⁄₁₆"

These are the settings on the pasta maker that I use. If I need a sheet to a #5 setting, I run the sheet through a #1, then a #3, and finally a #5. Remember to flatten the clay somewhat before you run it through the pasta maker. It will go through a lot easier.

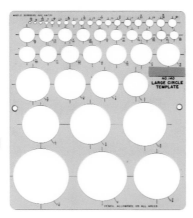

Circle template—The best way to accurately measure your clay balls. I just can't live without mine. Luckily, I married a mechanical engineer, or I may have never discovered this handy tool. You can find them at stationery stores, college bookstores, and on the Internet.

Cutters—Kemper Tools manufactures many different sizes and shapes of cutters. I press half of a circle cutter into the face to make perfect smiles every time. Cookie cutters are also great inspiration for your polymer clay creations.

Oven—If you are consistently baking a lot of polymer clay, you may want to consider getting a toaster oven or, better still, a convection oven. It's best if you keep your polymer clay away from your cooking.

Oven thermometer—To make sure the temperature on the dial is the actual temperature inside the oven.

Straight pins—To increase stability, put a straight pin or a 1" length of 18-gauge wire into your figurine before you attach the head.

Texture tools—Kitchen grater, texture plates, pieces of a screen, and rubber stamps are great to transform the polymer clay from a smooth surface.

Adhesives—E6000, cyanoacrylate adhesive.

Blush, chalk, eye shadow, and cotton swabs—Use to color unbaked polymer clay. Cotton swabs are used to apply the blush, chalk, and eye shadow.

Ruler—For measuring balls of clay, if you don't have a circle template. It is also great for measuring the length of logs.

Acrylic paint—I've used all the brands out there: Delta Ceramcoat, DecoArt Americana, and Plaid Folkart. Remember to use them only after the project has been baked.

Paintbrushes—I use a spotter brush for very detailed work, like making eyelashes. My main use for paintbrushes involves the blunt end. I use that for making holes. I have them in all sizes and most have never seen paint.

Quilt batting—Lay your pens on the quilt batting to bake. It will keep them from getting flat spots. Make sure the batting is not touching a side of the oven or the heating element.

Lame—For hanging ornaments.

Coffee cup—For propping figurines when baking. This keeps them from falling over. Ceramic or glass works well. Never use Styrofoam.

Basic Shapes

Cone

Egg

Teardrop

Log

Tapered log

Projects

These projects have been broken down into easy-to-follow steps. Watch your confidence grow as you finish a project. Just let your creativity go wild. Don't be afraid to make a mistake. Polymer clay is easy to work with. If you don't like the shape or look, just roll it into a ball and start again.

Add your own personal touch. The instructions are only guidelines. Don't be afraid to, as they say in the art world, "color outside the lines." The more you play with the clay and practice, the better you will become. I can't wait to see what you create!

Candy Cane Log

materials

• Premo! Sculpey: white, cadmium red

The candy cane log is used in the Fireman and the Ginger and Fred Christmas Ornaments projects. It is a very simple log to make. You can make candy canes out of extra clay.

1. Roll one ball each of white and cadmium red polymer clay, equal in size. Roll into logs.

2. Twist the logs together.

3. Continue twisting and reducing the log at the same time. Press and pull on the log as you are twisting until you have the log the size you want.

Babies and Blanket

This project idea actually came from my mother, Vivian Seyller. She was attending a baby shower for a relative who was expecting twin girls. Instead of the usual gifts, she wanted to give something special. Mom and I were pleased at how well this turned out. Some of my best designs have come from requests. They often take me in a direction I never thought I would go.

materials

- Granitex: 2 blocks of red
- Premo! Sculpey: white, black, ultramarine blue, beige, ecru, cadmium red, raw sienna, purple lavender—mix 1" ball of white with ½" ball of purple
- Brown paint
- Spotter paintbrush
- ⅜" Kemper circle cutter
- Small piece of cloth with some texture
- Pink blush or chalk
- Cotton swab
- Straight pin or 1" piece of 18-gauge wire
- Toothpick
- Pasta maker or acrylic brayer

Rug

1. Roll a 1⅛" ball of ultramarine blue Sculpey into a ⅛" thick log.

2. Place the ends together and twist. Curl the log into a circular rug shape.

For each Baby

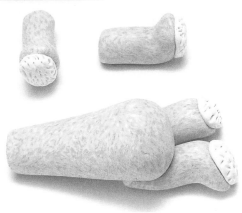

1. Body. Roll a ¹³⁄₁₆" ball of red Granitex into a 1" long tapered log.

2. Legs. Roll two ½" balls of red Granitex into ¾" long logs. Press one end of each log on a flat surface, and shape the end into a foot.

3. Pads. Roll two ¼" balls of white, and flatten them into ovals. Press one oval on the end of each foot. Use a toothpick to texture the pads.

4. Flatten the narrow end of each leg and press to the widest end of the body. Make sure that the feet are facing down.

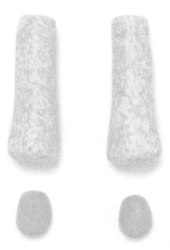

5. Arms. Roll two ½" balls of red Granitex into 1" long tapered logs.

6. Hands. Roll two ⁷⁄₃₂" balls of beige into teardrops. Flatten and press one to the end of each arm.

7. Flatten the narrow end of each arm and press one onto each side of the body. Bend each arm to create an elbow. It will look like the baby is lying on her elbows. Press a wire halfway into the top of the body to stabilize the head.

8. Head. Roll a ¾" ball of beige.

9. Nose. Roll a ¹⁄₁₆" ball of beige. Press it on the center of the head.

10. Mouth. Use a circle cutter to make the mouth.

11. Use the cotton swab to apply blush to the cheeks.

12. Ears. Roll two ⅛" balls of beige into ovals. Press one onto each side of the head. Use a toothpick to make two lines in each ear.

13. Hair. Roll a ³⁄₁₆" ball of raw sienna into a 4" long log. Pile the hair loosely into a ball, and press it to the top of the head.

14. Place the head on top of the body.

15. Repeat steps 1–14 for the second baby. Place the babies on the rug.

Blanket

1. Flatten a sheet of lavender along with a piece of cloth at a #4 setting on the pasta maker. The texture of the cloth will transfer to the clay. Cut it into a 2" by 1⅛" rectangle.

2. Fringe. Use a knife to make ½" cuts along the narrowest sides.

3. Place the blanket between the babies.

Bear

1. Body. Roll a ⅜" ball of raw sienna into a cone. Flatten slightly.

2. Legs. Roll two 7/32" balls of raw sienna into ⅜" long logs. Press them to the body.

3. Arms. Roll two 7/32" balls of raw sienna into ½" long logs. Press them to the body.

4. Head. Roll a ⅜" ball of raw sienna into an oval and flatten slightly.

5. Snout. Roll a ⅛" ball of ecru and flatten. Press it to the head.

6. Nose. Roll a 1/16" ball of black and press it to the snout.

7. Eyes. Use a toothpick to make two holes for the eyes.

8. Ears. Roll two ⅛" balls of raw sienna into ¼" long logs. Fold them in half and press them to the head. Press the head to the top of the body.

9. Place the bear on the blanket.

10. Bake and let cool.

Eyes on babies

After the piece has baked and cooled, use brown paint to make half-circle eyes on each baby.

Chocolate Kiss Guy

materials

- Premo! Sculpey: burnt umber, beige, white, black
- 2" square piece of aluminum foil
- E6000 glue
- 5/16" Kemper circle cutter
- Pink blush or chalk
- Cotton swab

My home is rarely without chocolate kisses, so it is no mystery where the inspiration came for this little guy. Can I stop at eating just one? Just one bag, sure! The best part of this chocolate kiss is that he is non-fattening.

1. **Body.** Roll a 1" ball of burnt umber into the shape of the kiss, about 2" tall. Curl the tip.

2. **Face.** Roll a ⅜" ball of beige into an oval and flatten it. Press it to the body.

3. **Eyes.** Roll two ³⁄₃₂" balls of white into teardrops and flatten. Press the narrow ends together, and press them to the face.

4. **Pupils.** Roll two ¹⁄₃₂" balls of black. Flatten and press one onto each eye.

5. **Eyebrows.** Roll two ³⁄₃₂" balls of beige into tapered logs and press around the top of each eye.

6. **Nose.** Roll a ³⁄₃₂" ball of beige, and press it to the face.

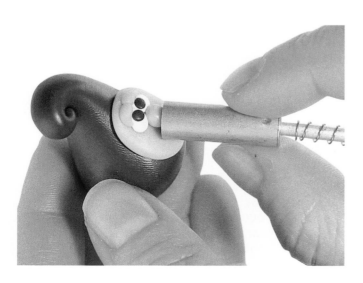

7. For the mouth, use the circle cutter. Use the cotton swab to apply blush to the cheeks.

8. Bake and cool.

9. Press aluminum foil around the kiss. Remove the foil, place some glue on the bottom of the kiss, and replace the foil.

Clown

materials

- Premo! Sculpey: cobalt blue (2 blocks), fluorescent green, white, orange, black, beige, cadmium red, fluorescent pink, fuchsia, purple, cadmium yellow
  lavender—mix a ³⁄₁₆" ball of white with a ¹⁄₁₆" ball of purple
- 2 black seed beads
- 6" of 24-gauge red Fun Wire
- Straight pin or 1" piece of 18-gauge wire
- Toothpick
- ¼" Kemper flower cutter
- Pasta maker or acrylic brayer

I grew up watching Bozo the Clown on television. I longed to be chosen to play "The Grand Prize Game," where you dropped ping-pong balls into buckets to win prizes. Clowns have always fascinated me. They come in all shapes and sizes, every color in the rainbow, and every facial expression one could imagine. This project is bound to put a smile on your face.

1. Body. Roll a 1⅛" ball of cobalt blue into a cone. Roll three ⅛" balls each of fluorescent green, orange, fluorescent pink, and cadmium yellow. Flatten and press the balls randomly all over the body. Press a wire halfway into the top of the body to stabilize the head.

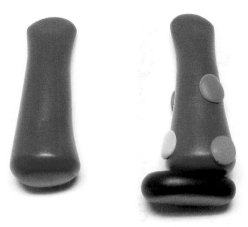

5. Hands. Roll two ¼" balls of beige into teardrops. Flatten slightly and press one to the end of each arm.

2. Legs. Roll two ¹¹⁄₁₆" balls of cobalt blue into 1¼" long tapered logs. Roll two ⅛" balls each of fluorescent green, orange, fluorescent pink, and cadmium yellow. Flatten and press one of each color randomly over each leg.

3. Shoes. Roll two ½" balls of black. Flatten them into ovals and press one to the end of each leg. Flatten the narrow end of each leg. Press one leg to each side of the body. When the leg is attached, make sure that the widest end of the shoe is on the top part of the leg.

6. Ball. Roll a ⅞" ball of purple. Use a toothpick to draw lines around ball.

4. Arms. Roll two ⅝" balls of cobalt blue into 1¼" long tapered logs. Roll two ⅛" balls each of fluorescent green, orange, fluorescent pink, and cadmium yellow. Flatten and press one of each color randomly over each arm. Press the arms to both sides of the body. Make sure they line up with the top of the body.

7. Place the ball in the clown's hands.

8. Collar. Gradually flatten a sheet of white through the pasta maker, using setting #1, #3, and finally #5. This makes it a lot easier to run through the pasta machine. Cut a ⅜" by 4" rectangle. Pleat the rectangle into a circle, and press it to the top of the body.

9. **Head.** Roll a $^{13}/_{16}$" ball of beige into an oval.

10. **Eyes.** Roll two $^{3}/_{16}$" balls of white. Flatten them into ovals, and press them to the head. Roll two $^{1}/_{4}$" balls of lavender, and flatten them into circles. Press a lavender circle onto each eye. Use a toothpick to press a seed bead into each eye.

11. **Eyebrows.** Roll two $^{1}/_{32}$" diameter black logs. Press one around the top half of each eye.

12. **Nose.** Roll a $^{3}/_{16}$" ball of cadmium red into an oval. Press it to the head.

13. **Mouth.** Roll a $^{1}/_{4}$" ball of cadmium red, and flatten it into the shape of a smile. Press it to the head, and use a toothpick to draw the opening of the mouth.

14. **Ears.** Roll two $^{1}/_{8}$" balls of beige into ovals. Press one ear to each side of the head. Make sure they are even with each other. Use a toothpick to make two lines in each ear.

15. **Hat.** For the brim, roll a $^{7}/_{16}$" ball of fluorescent green and flatten it into a circle. Press it to the top of the head. Roll a $^{9}/_{16}$" ball of fluorescent green into a cylinder and press it to the top of the brim. Cut two 3" lengths of the red wire. Wrap each wire around the paintbrush to make a coil. Roll one sheet each of fuchsia and cadmium yellow through the pasta maker to a #5 setting. Use the flower cutter to cut out two fuchsia and two cadmium yellow flowers. Place one end of each wire between the two fuchsia flowers and press together. Do the same with the cadmium yellow flowers. Press the wires into the top of the hat.

Firefighter

It takes a special kind of person to be a fireman. The dedication and fearlessness that they bring to their jobs is often thankless. This character is in appreciation of those who fight to save lives every day. I saw a bumper sticker the other day that really sums it all up: "I fight what you fear."

materials

- Premo! Sculpey: black (2 blocks), cadmium yellow, beige, raw sienna, ultramarine blue, white, cadmium red
  gray—mix a ½" ball of black with a ¼" ball of white
- 2 black seed beads
- Yellow paint
- White paint
- Spotter paintbrush
- Pink blush or chalk
- Cotton swab
- Straight pin or 1" piece of 18-gauge wire
- ¾" Kemper heart cutter
- Pasta machine or acrylic brayer

Heart

1. Roll a sheet of ultramarine blue through the pasta maker at a #1 setting. Use the heart cutter to cut out one heart.

2. Roll a ⅜" ball each of white and cadmium red. Roll each color into a log. Twist the two logs together. Continue to roll and twist the logs into a single ³⁄₃₂" thick log. Press the log around the heart. Use a knife to cut off any excess so that the ends meet. Bake.

3. When cooled, use white paint to write "U.S.A." on the heart. Set aside.

Firefighter

1. Body. Roll a 1" ball of black into a cone. Press a wire halfway into the top of the body to stabilize the head.

2. Legs. Roll two ⅝" balls of black into 1" long tapered logs. Flatten the narrowest end slightly.

3. Stripes. Roll a sheet of cadmium yellow through the pasta maker to a #5 setting. Cut a ⅛" wide strip. Wrap a piece of the strip around the end of each leg. Set the sheet aside to use later.

5. Arms. Roll two ⁹⁄₁₆" balls of black into 1¼" long tapered logs. Flatten the narrowest end slightly.

6. Stripes. Wrap a yellow strip around the wide end of each arm and ¾" up from the first stripe. Flatten the narrow end of each arm, and press one arm onto each side of the body. Make sure the arms line up with the top of the body.

4. Shoes. Roll two ⁵⁄₁₆" balls of gray. Flatten slightly and press one to the end of each leg. Roll two ⅜" balls of gray, and flatten them into ovals. Press one to the end of each leg. Use the side of a paintbrush to roll up and down the bottom of each shoe. Flatten the narrow end of each leg. Press one leg to each side of the body. When the leg is attached, make sure that the widest end of the shoe is on the top part of the leg.

7. Hands. Roll two ¼" balls of beige into teardrops. Flatten slightly and press to the widest end of each arm.

8. Collar. Roll a sheet of black through the pasta maker to a #5 setting. Cut two rectangles, ⅛" by ½". Press the two rectangles to the body with corners together.

9. Use a knife to draw a line down the center of the body.

10. Buttons. Use a toothpick to make dots down each side of the line.

11. Stripes. Cut six ⅛" by ⅜" rectangles. Place three on the front of body.

12. Position the heart in the hands.

13. Place three rectangles on the back of the body.

14. **Head.** Roll a ⅞" ball of beige.

15. **Eyes.** Press two seed beads into the head. Use a toothpick to make two squint lines by each eye. Use the cotton swab to apply blush to the cheeks.

16. **Hair.** Roll two ⁵⁄₁₆" balls of raw sienna into teardrops. Flatten the teardrops, and press them to the head, crossing the points in front.

17. **Ears.** Roll two ⅛" balls of beige. Press the ears to both sides of the head. Make sure they are even with each other. Use a toothpick to make two lines in each ear.

18. **Hat**. Roll a ⁹⁄₁₆" ball of black, and flatten it into a circle. Place the circle on the head to create a rim for the hat. Roll a ⁹⁄₁₆" ball of black into a ¾" long tapered log. Shape the log into a triangle. Use the toothpick to make dots around the front of the hat. Place the hat on top of the rim.

19. Place the head on top of the body. Bake. After the firefighter has cooled, use yellow paint to write "FD" on the front of the hat.

Ladybug and Clay Pot

materials

- Premo! Sculpey: black, cadmium red, white, cadmium yellow, orange
- 3" clay pot
- "Let It Bloom" Polyform Products flexible push mold
- 2 black seed beads
- 7" of 24-gauge black Fun Wire
- Straight pin or 1" piece of 18-gauge wire
- 2 ceramic or glass coffee cups, for propping
- Paintbrush, for twisting wire
- 1½" heart cookie cutter
- 7/16" Kemper circle cutter
- E6000 glue

The past few summers we have been invaded by millions of ladybugs. Of course, the experts call them Japanese beetles. To me, they are ladybugs, so it's no wonder they inspired this project. I must thank Dawn Kaltenhauser of Blumenhaus Florist in Stillwater, Minnesota, for the flower arrangement.

Flowers

1. Using the push mold, press a ball of orange clay into the center of the flower mold just until it is even with the petals. Press a ball of cadmium yellow clay into the center of the flower covering the orange. Press from the center out, filling in all the petals.

2. Pop out the flower. Make 11 to 13 flowers.

3. Bake and set aside.

Ladybug

1. Body. Roll a ⅞" ball of black into a cone.

2. Arms. Roll two ⅜" balls of black into 1" tapered logs. Press one onto each side of the body and curl them because they will be hanging over the clay pot.

11. Antenna. Cut two ½" lengths of black wire, and press them into the top of the head. Roll two ⅛" balls of black, and press one on top of each wire. Press a wire halfway into the top of the body to stabilize the head. Press the head to the top of the body.

12. Wings. Roll a sheet of red through the pasta maker to a #5 setting. Use the heart cookie cutter to cut out the heart.

13. Spots. Roll eight ⅛" balls of black. Flatten them slightly, and press them randomly all over the heart.

3. Legs. Cut two 3" long lengths of black wire. Wrap each wire around the paintbrush to coil.

4. Feet. Roll two ¼" balls of black into ovals and flatten slightly.

5. Press one end of the coiled wire leg into each foot, and then press the other end of each leg into the bottom of the body.

6. Head. Roll a ⅝" ball of black.

7. Face. Roll a ¼" ball of white, and flatten it to a ⁷⁄₁₆" circle. Press it to the head.

8. Eyes. Press two black seed beads into the face. Use a toothpick to make two squint lines by each eye.

14. Set the clay pot on its side, and position the ladybug on the pot.

15. Press the wings upside down on the back of the ladybug, so the tip of the heart is pointed toward the head of the ladybug. Prop the ladybug and clay pot between two coffee cups to keep them from moving during baking. Bake.

9. Nose. Roll a ⅛" ball of red into an oval and press it under the eyes.

10. Mouth. Press half of a circle cutter into the face under the nose.

16. When cooled, glue the ladybug to the pot, and glue the flowers randomly all over the pot.

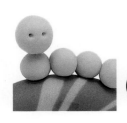

Snail and Friend Eraser

materials

- Amazing Eraser Clay—pink, purple, mango, and green
- New yellow pencil
- Toothpick

This project uses a new clay called Amazing Eraser Clay. The clay is wonderfully soft and easy to work with. It bakes in the oven at 250 degrees for 10 minutes, and when it comes out you have an eraser. I know I can never have too many erasers.

This is a great project for kids. But if it is going to be used for an actual eraser, the worm may not stay on.

Snail

1. Shell. Roll ⅞" balls each of pink and purple into logs. Twist the logs together, and roll them into a ball. Roll the ball into a 7½" long log, twisting the log as you roll it out.

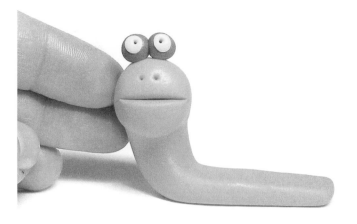

2. Curl the log into a shell, and flatten the bottom.

3. Body. Roll a ⅞" ball of pink into a 1½" long tapered log. Flatten the narrowest half of the log, and curl the wider end around into a neck and head.

4. Eyes. Roll two ⁷⁄₃₂" balls of purple. Press them together slightly. Roll two ¹⁄₁₆" balls of mango, and flatten them. Press the mango circles to the front of each eye.

5. Pupil. Use a toothpick to make a hole in each eye.

6. Mouth. Use a knife to make a mouth.

7. Nose. Make two holes above the mouth for nostrils.

8. Press the shell to the flattened part of the body. Make a hole in the bottom of body, large enough for a pencil top to fit in but not too large that the eraser will wobble.

Worm

1. Head. Roll a ¼" ball of green. Use a toothpick to make two holes for the eyes.

2. Body. Roll four ³⁄₁₆" balls of green. Press all the balls together. Place the worm body on the snail.

3. Press the head of the worm onto its body.

Wacky Bird

materials

- Premo! Sculpey: violet, fluorescent green, orange, cadmium yellow, white, black, fluorescent pink
- 2¼" of 24-gauge black Fun Wire
- Straight pin or 1" piece of 18-gauge wire

I love the 1960s. It might have to do with the fact that I was born then. It was the time of wild and vivid colors. The more the colors clashed, the better. This project shows you not to be afraid to use color. You can't go wrong.

1. Body. Roll a 1" ball of violet. Roll fifteen ³⁄₃₂" balls of fluorescent pink. Flatten the pink balls slightly, and press them randomly all over body.

2. Neck. Roll a ³⁄₈" ball of fluorescent green, and flatten it slightly. Place it on top of the body. Press a wire halfway into the top of the body to stabilize the head.

3. Head. Roll an ¹¹⁄₁₆" ball of fluorescent green.

4. Beak. Roll a ¼" ball of cadmium yellow. Flatten the yellow ball, and press it to the head.

6. Eyes. Roll two ³⁄₁₆" balls of white. Press them together, and place them on the head.

7. Pupils. Roll two ¹⁄₃₂" balls of black. Flatten them slightly, and press one onto each eye.

8. Hairs. Cut three ¾" long pieces of black wire. Curl over one end of each, and press the other end into the top of the head.

5. Nose. Roll a ³⁄₈" ball of cadmium yellow into a ¾" long cone. Press it to the head, and bend it down.

9. Roll eight ³⁄₃₂" balls of fluorescent pink. Flatten them slightly, and press them randomly all over the head. Press the head to the top of the body.

10. Wings. Roll two ⁹⁄₁₆" balls of violet into teardrops and flatten slightly. Use a knife to feather each wing. Press the wings to the body making sure they are even with each other.

11. Feet. Roll two ³⁄₈" balls of orange. Flatten and shape them into teardrops. Use a knife to make three toes in each foot. Press the feet to the bottom of the body.

Pen Projects

Covering pens with polymer clay is one of the most fun things to do. In fact, a giraffe pen I created and sent to a craft magazine began my transition into being a designer. A simple layer of polymer clay around the pen is your canvas. The possibilities are endless.

How to Cover a Pen with Polymer Clay

1. Use pliers to remove the ink cartridge from the pen. If you leave the ink cartridge inside the pen it will melt during baking and create quite a mess.

2. Roll a sheet of polymer clay through the pasta maker at a #1 setting.

3. Cut the sheet to fit around the pen.

4. Use your fingers to smooth out the seam.

5. Roll the pen against a flat surface to even the clay.

*H*umpty Dumpty Pen

materials

- Premo! Scupley: white (2 blocks), cadmium yellow, black, cobalt blue, cadmium red
  gray—mix one 2 oz. block of white with 1½ block of black
  light blue—mix a 3/16" ball of white with a ⅛" ball of blue
- Bic® round stick pen
- 14" of 24-gauge black Fun Wire
- 6" scrap of quilt batting
- Paintbrush for indenting the eggs
- Shade-Tex Architecture Rubbing Plates, small brick sheet
- ⁷⁄₁₆" Kemper circle cutter
- Pasta maker or acrylic brayer

Please, review "How to Cover a Pen with Polymer Clay," page 29, before beginning this project.

I love those old nursery rhymes from my childhood. This one just seemed perfect for a pen project. My husband, Curt, thought this pen would crack you up. He is quite a character.

Pen

1. Cover the pen with gray polymer clay.

2. Roll the pen against the brick sheet to texture the pen. You can also use a knife to draw bricks around the pen.

3. **Egg whites.** Roll six ⅜" balls of white, and flatten them to ⅝" round. Indent the sides of each egg white four times using a paintbrush. Press the egg whites randomly around the pen.

4. **Egg yolks.** Roll six ³⁄₁₆" balls of cadmium yellow. Flatten the balls slightly, and press one in the center of each egg white. Set the pen aside on quilt batting.

Humpty Dumpty

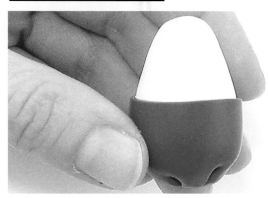

1. **Body.** Roll a 1" ball of white into an egg shape. Roll a sheet of cobalt blue through the pasta maker to a #5 setting. Cut a 1" strip of cadmium blue, and wrap it around the lower half of the egg, matching up the seams. Use a knife to trim the extra clay and smooth the blue into the egg around the bottom. Press the bottom against a smooth surface to flatten it.

2. **Eyes.** Roll two ⅛" balls of light blue. Flatten them into ovals, and press them to the egg. Roll two balls of white, slightly larger than ¹⁄₁₆". Flatten them, and press one to the bottom half of each eye. Roll two ¹⁄₁₆" balls of black. Flatten them, and press one to the white of each eye.

3. **Nose.** Roll a ³⁄₁₆" ball of white, and press it to the egg under the eyes.

4. **Mouth.** Press half of the circle cutter into the egg under the nose to make the mouth.

5. **Bow.** Roll two ³⁄₁₆" balls of red. Flatten the red balls into triangles. Use a toothpick to press a line into the middle of each triangle. Press the pointed ends of the two triangles together to make a bow, and press the bow to the egg. Roll a ⅛" ball of red, and press it to the center of the bow.

6. **Legs.** Cut two 4" lengths of black wire. Coil each wire around a paintbrush.

7. **Feet.** Roll two ⅜" balls of black, and flatten them slightly. Press one end of each wire into the center of a foot, and place the other end into the lower part of the egg.

8. **Arms.** Cut two 3" lengths of black wire. Wrap each wire around a paintbrush to coil.

9. **Hands.** Roll two ⁵⁄₁₆" balls of red. Flatten each ball slightly into a teardrop.

10. **Thumb.** Roll two ⅛" balls of red into teardrops. Press one to the side of each hand. Place one end of wire into the bottom of each hand, and press the other end into the side of the body.

11. Press Humpty Dumpty to the top of the pen. Before you bake, make sure he is lying on some quilt batting to prevent flat spots.

12. For stability, remove Humpty Dumpty from the pen after he is baked and cooled. Apply glue to the top of the pen, and place him back on. Press the ink cartridge back into the pen.

Jester Pen

Jesters were slaves of wealthy men back in medieval days. Their job was to entertain. This pen is covered with balloons, and the jester is just waiting to see what kind of trouble he can get into.

materials

- Premo! Sculpey: orange, cobalt blue (2 blocks), beige, green, cadmium yellow, cadmium red, raw sienna, fluorescent pink, fuchsia, purple
- Bic round stick pen
- 2 black seed beads
- 6" scrap of quilt batting
- Paintbrush
- 7/16" Kemper circle cutter
- Pasta maker or acrylic brayer

Please, review "How to Cover a Pen with Polymer Clay," page 29, before beginning this project.

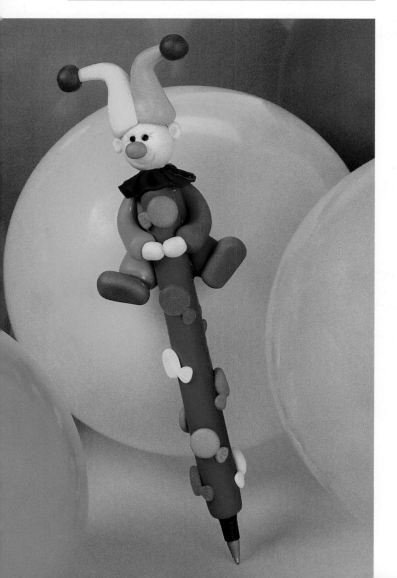

Pen

1. Cover the pen with cobalt blue.

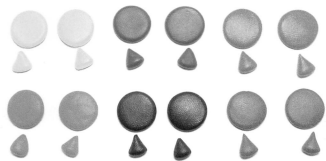

2. Balloons. Roll two 5/16" and two 3/16" balls each of cadmium red, fluorescent pink, fluorescent yellow, orange, purple, and green.

3. Flatten the 5/16" balls to 1/2" wide circles. Flatten the 3/16" balls into triangles.

4. Place the flattened balls randomly all over the pen. Place the triangles randomly around each ball, so it looks like the balloons are going all different ways. Use a knife to make three lines in each triangle.

Clown

1. **Body and Legs.** Roll a ⅞" ball of each green and fuchsia. Roll each ball into a 2¼" long tapered log. Press the narrow ends of the logs together.

2. **Shoes.** Roll two ½" balls of raw sienna into ovals. Flatten the balls, and press the shoes to the bottom of each leg.

3. Press the upper body to the pen, making sure the top of the body is even with the top of the pen. Then curl each leg around both sides of the pen.

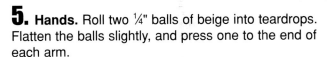

4. **Arms.** Roll a ⅝" ball of each green and fuchsia. Roll the balls into 1½" long tapered logs. Press the arms to the body. Make sure the tops of the arms are even with the top of the body. Curl each arm around the pen so that the arms are holding the pen.

5. **Hands.** Roll two ¼" balls of beige into teardrops. Flatten the balls slightly, and press one to the end of each arm.

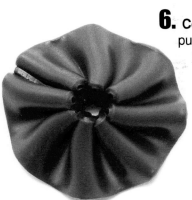

6. **Collar.** Roll a sheet of purple through the pasta maker to a #5 setting. Cut a ½" by 4" rectangle. Pleat the rectangle into a circle, and press it to the top of the body.

7. **Head.** Roll a ¹³⁄₁₆" ball of beige.

8. **Eyes.** Press two seed beads into the head. Use a toothpick to make two squint lines by each eye.

9. **Nose.** Roll a ⁷⁄₃₂" ball of cadmium red into an oval. Press the nose to the face below the eyes.

10. **Mouth.** Use a circle cutter to make the mouth.

11. **Ears.** Roll two ³⁄₁₆" balls of beige. Press one ear to each side of the the head. Use the blunt end of the paintbrush to make a hole in each ear.

12. **Hat.** Roll ¹¹⁄₁₆" balls of each cadmium yellow and orange into 2" long tapered logs. Press the logs together with the narrower ends pointing out. Roll two ⅜" balls of purple. Make a hole in each ball, and press the narrow end of each log into each ball. Press around the ball to seal any gaps left by the holes.

13. Press the hat to the top of the head, and then press the head to the top of the body.

14. Before your bake, make sure the jester is lying on some quilt batting to prevent flat spots.

15. When cooled, press the ink cartridge back into the pen.

Sea Life Pen

A pen is a great place to create an underwater scene. This pen has fish and octopuses along with a dolphin to top it off. You could have sharks, sponges, sea stars, and crabs. The possibilities are as endless as the sea itself. I like to use this pen during those long cold Minnesota winters. It reminds me of the Hawaiian vacations we've taken.

Pen

Cover the pen with Granitex blue.

Fish

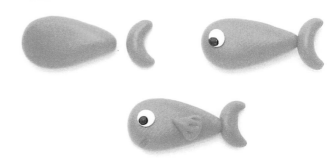

1. Fish body. Roll a ³⁄₈" ball of orange into a ¾" long teardrop and flatten slightly.

2. Tail fin. Roll a ³⁄₁₆" ball of orange into a ½" long log, tapering both ends. Curl the log slightly into a "C" shape, and press the tail to the end of the body.

3. Eye. Roll a ¹⁄₁₆" ball of white, and press it to the body.

4. Pupil. Roll a ¹⁄₃₂" ball of black, and press it to the eye.

5. Dorsal fin. Roll a ⅛" ball of orange into a teardrop. Flatten the teardrop slightly, and press it to the body.

6. Use a knife to make three lines in the fin. Use the knife to make a mouth.

7. Make an ultramarine fish and a purple fish.

Octopus

1. Octopus body. Roll a ⅜" ball of green, and flatten it into a ⁷⁄₁₆" wide circle.

2. Eyes. Roll two ¹⁄₁₆" balls of white. Flatten them, and press them to the body.

3. Pupils. Roll two ¹⁄₃₂" balls of black, and press them to the eyes.

4. Mouth. Use a circle cutter to make a mouth.

5. Tentacles. Roll four ³⁄₃₂" balls of green into ½" long tapered logs. Pile the logs together, and curl the ends slightly to one side. Press the tentacles to the bottom of the body.

6. Make a yellow octopus and fuchsia octopus.

7. Press the fish and octopuses randomly all over pen.

Dolphin

1. Dolphin Body. Roll a 1" ball of gray into a 2¾" long tapered log. Shape the narrow end into a tail. Shape the other end into a head.

2. Eyes. Press two seed beads into the head. Use a toothpick to make two squint lines in each eye.

3. Mouth. Use a knife to make the mouth.

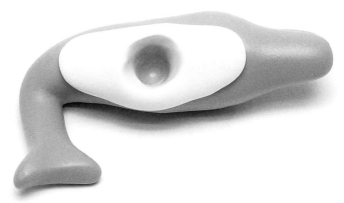

4. Stomach. Roll a ⁷⁄₁₆" ball of white into a 1" long oval. Flatten the oval, and press it to the underside of the dolphin. Curl the tail to the side. Use the end of a paintbrush to make a hole in the bottom of the dolphin large enough for the pen top to fit snugly.

5. Fin. Roll a ⁵⁄₁₆" ball of gray, and flatten it into a teardrop. Flatten the bottom of the teardrop to form a fin shape. Press the fin to the top of the dolphin, centering it on the body. Press the dolphin to the top of the pen.

6. Before your bake, make sure the dolphin is lying on some quilt batting to prevent flat spots. When cooled, press the ink cartridge back into the pen.

The Holiday Projects

Holidays are a great source for characters made of polymer clay. I have always loved making gifts for my family and friends using this medium. Can you ever have too many Christmas ornaments?

One of my first experiences with polymer clay was making pumpkins. I have made them in all shapes and sizes. Pumpkins lead the way to ghosts, Santas, bunnies, and thousands of others. Give it a try and see for yourself.

$\mathcal{S}$weet Heart

This little character wants to be your sweetheart this Valentine's Day. She doesn't want candy or cards. She just wants to be set in a special place. What's not to love?

materials

• Premo! Sculpey: cadmium red, white, black pink—mix a ⅜" ball of white with a ⅛" ball of cadmium red
• 6" of 24-gauge black Fun Wire
• Paintbrush
• ¾" Kemper circle cutter
• ¼" and ³⁄₁₆" Kemper heart cutters
• E6000 glue

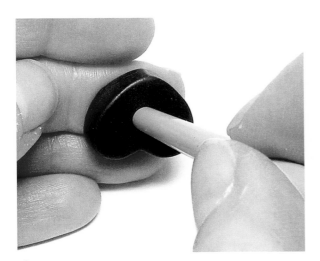

1. Feet. Flatten a 1" ball of black until it's ¼" thick. Use the ¾" heart cutter to cut out a heart. Use the end of a paintbrush to make a hole in the center of the heart. Bake and set aside.

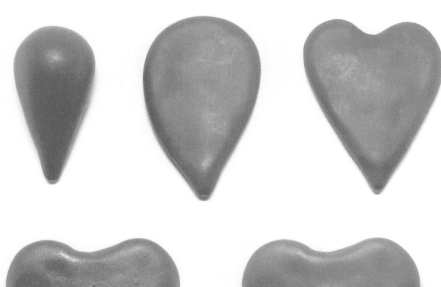

2. Body. Roll a 1" ball of cadmium red into a teardrop. Flatten the ball into the shape of a heart

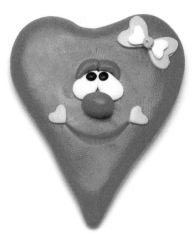

3. Eyes. Roll two ⅛" balls of white. Flatten them into teardrops, and press them to the heart.

4. Pupils. Roll two ¹⁄₃₂" balls of black, and press them to the eyes.

5. Eyebrows. Roll two ⅛" balls of cadmium red into tapered logs. Curve the logs slightly, and press one above each eye.

6. Nose. Roll a ⁷⁄₃₂" ball of cadmium red into an oval. Press it to the heart below the eyes.

7. Mouth. Use the circle cutter to make the mouth.

8. Hearts. Roll a sheet of white and then a sheet of pink through the pasta maker to a #5 setting. Use heart cutters to cut out two ³⁄₁₆" hearts in both pink and white. Also cut out two ¼" hearts in pink. Press the ³⁄₁₆" pink hearts to both ends of the mouth.

9. Bow. Using the remaining hearts, press the ¼" pink hearts onto the red heart with the pointed ends touching, and then press the ³⁄₁₆" white hearts over the pink hearts. Roll a ¹⁄₁₆" ball of pink, and press it into the center of the bow. Use a toothpick to indent the pink ball.

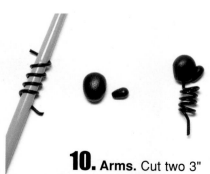

10. Arms. Cut two 3" long lengths of the black wire. Wrap each wire around a paintbrush to coil.

11. Hands. Roll two ¼" balls of black into ovals, and flatten them slightly.

12. Thumbs. Roll two ⅛" balls of black into teardrops, and press them on each side of the hands. Press one end of the coiled wire into each hand, and then press each arm into the side of the heart.

13. Bake the heart and let cool. Glue the heart to the feet.

Bunny and Chick Easter Eggs

Easter is associated with brightly colored eggs, bunnies, baby chicks, and, of course, candy. This project incorporates several Easter symbols. Enjoy decorating your egg in bright springtime colors.

materials

For each
• 4 black seed beads
• Pink blush or chalk
• Cotton swab
• Toothpick

For the Bunny Egg
• Premo! Sculpey: violet, fluorescent pink, fluorescent yellow, white
  pink—mix a ¼" ball of white with a ¹⁄₁₆" ball of cadmium red

For the Chick Egg
• Premo! Sculpey: ultramarine blue, fluorescent green, fluorescent pink, cadmium yellow, orange

Bunny Egg

1. Egg. Roll a 1⅛" ball of violet into an egg shape. Roll a ½" ball of fluorescent pink into a ¹⁄₁₆" thick log. Randomly run the log all over the egg. Roll ¹⁄₁₆" balls of fluorescent yellow, and press them all over the egg.

2. **Head.** Roll a ¾" ball of white.

3. **Eyes.** Press two black seed beads into the head. Use a toothpick to make two squint lines by each eye.

4. **Muzzle.** Roll two ¼" balls of white. Flatten them slightly, and place them on the head.

5. **Nose.** Roll a ¹⁄₁₆" ball of pink. Place it in the center of the muzzle. Use a cotton swab to apply blush to the cheeks. Press the head to the top of the egg.

6. **Arms.** Roll two ⁷⁄₁₆" balls of white into 1" long logs. Flatten one end slightly and round off the other end. Press the arms to the egg and curl them around to the front of the egg. Make sure the tops of the arms are even with the top of the egg.

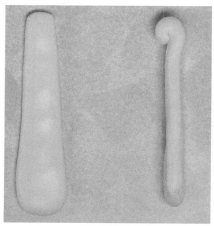

7. **Ears.** Roll two ½" balls of white and flatten each into a floppy ear shape. Each ear should measure about 1¾" long. Turn over the top end of each ear, and press one ear onto each side of the head.

8. **Feet.** Roll two ½" balls of white, and shape them into feet. Use a toothpick to make three paw lines.

9. **Pads.** Roll two ³⁄₁₆" balls of pink. Flatten the balls into ovals, and place one on each foot. Roll six ¹⁄₁₆" balls of pink, and press three above each oval. Press each foot onto the egg.

Chick Egg

1. **Egg.** Refer to Bunny Egg Step 1, except use ultramarine blue for the egg, fluorescent green for the log, and fluorescent pink for the tiny balls.

2. **Head.** Roll a ¾" ball of cadmium yellow.

3. **Eyes.** Press two black seed beads into the head. Use a toothpick to make two squint lines by each eye.

4. **Beak.** Roll a ¼" ball of orange into a cone. Press it onto the head. Use a knife to cut halfway through the beak, and separate it slightly.

5. Press the head onto the top of the egg.

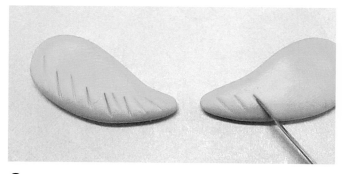

6. **Wings.** Roll two ½" balls of cadmium yellow, and shape them into teardrops. Use a knife to make feather lines on each wing. Press a wing on each side of the egg and curve it to the front of the egg. Make sure the tops of the wings are even with the top of the egg.

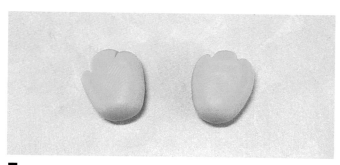

7. **Feet.** Roll two ⁷⁄₁₆" balls of cadmium yellow, and flatten them into the shape of feet. Use a knife to make two lines in each foot.

8. Press the feet onto the egg.

Halloween Pumpkin Cat and Ghost

materials

- Premo! Sculpey
  pumpkin: orange (2 blocks)
  cat: black, white, cadmium red
  pink—mix a ⅜" ball of white with a ⅛" ball of
    cadmium red
  ghost: white
- 4 wiggle eyes, 5 mm
- ⅜" Kemper round cutter
- Straight pin or 1" piece of 18-gauge wire
- Pink blush or chalk
- Cotton swab
- Toothpick
- E6000 glue

How about something different this Halloween? This project may look tricky but it is really quite simple. Instead of candy for your special friends and family members, these characters are sure to please everyone. They last a lot longer than candy, and they won't give you a stomachache.

Pumpkin Body

1. Roll a 1⅛" ball of orange

2. Use a toothpick to make lines all around the pumpkin. Press a wire halfway into the top of the body to stabilize the head.

Cat

1. Head. Roll a 9/16" ball of black, and flatten it slightly. The shape will resemble a peppermint candy.

2. Snout. Roll two 1/4" balls of white. Flatten and press them together. Press the snout to the head.

3. Nose. Roll a 1/16" ball of pink, and press it on the center of the snout.

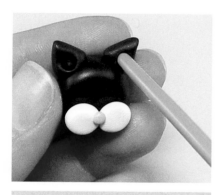

4. Ears. Roll two 7/32" balls of black. Flatten the balls into triangles. Press the ears to the head. Use the blunt end of paintbrush to make a hole in each ear. Press head onto top of pumpkin.

5. Upper Paws. Roll two 3/8" balls of black, and shape them into paws.

6. Pads. Roll two 1/8" balls of pink, flatten them, and press one onto each upper paw. Roll six 1/16" balls of pink, flatten them, and press three above each pad. Press the upper paws to the body.

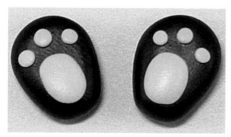

7. Lower Paws. Roll two 7/16" balls of black. Shape them into paws.

8. Pads. Roll two 3/32" balls of pink, flatten them, and press one onto each lower paw. Roll six 1/16" balls of pink, flatten them, and press three above each pad. Press the paws to the body.

9. Bake and let cool. Glue on the wiggle eyes.

Ghost

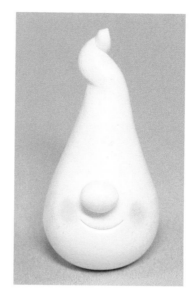

1. Head. Roll a 3/4" ball of white into a long cone. Twist the tip.

2. Nose. Roll a 3/32" ball of white, and press it to the head.

3. Mouth. Press half of the circle cutter into the head.

4. Use the cotton swab to apply blush to the cheeks. Press the head to the top of the pumpkin.

5. Hands. Roll two 7/16" balls of white. Flatten them into hands. Use a knife to make three fingers. Press the hands to the upper part of the pumpkin. Make sure they are even across from each other.

6. Feet. Roll two 1/2" balls of white into teardrops, and flatten them into feet. Press the feet to the pumpkin, making sure they are even with each other.

7. Bake and let cool. Glue on the wiggle eyes.

Thanksgiving Couple

materials

- Premo! Sculpey: white (3 blocks), orange, black, beige, ecru, gold, green, raw sienna, cadmium yellow
  gray—mix 2 blocks of white with a half block of black
- 4 black seed beads
- 1" piece of a window screen or mesh
- Straight pin or 1" piece of 18-gauge wire
- Pink blush or chalk
- Cotton swab
- Toothpick
- Paintbrush
- Pasta machine or acrylic brayer

Thanksgiving is a time to gather with family and friends. It's a time to eat too much turkey, too much stuffing, too much of everything. Sometimes we forget about the pilgrims who left England, fleeing religious persecution, to travel to the New World. They endured many hardships. I hope this project has you looking at Thanksgiving in a different way.

Pumpkin

1. Roll a ¾" ball of orange. Use a toothpick to make lines all around the pumpkin. Use the blunt end of a paintbrush to make a hole in the top.

2. Stem. Roll a ³⁄₁₆" ball of raw sienna into a teardrop. Flatten the wider end of the teardrop to form the stem, and the press the narrower end into the top of the pumpkin.

3. Tendrils. Roll two ⅛" balls of green into 1" long logs. Gently twist each log and set them on opposite sides of the pumpkin. Bake the pumpkin and set aside.

Corn

1. Roll two ⁵⁄₁₆" balls of cadmium yellow into ⁵⁄₈" long logs. Roll each log against the screen to create kernels on the corn.

2. Gradually flatten a sheet of ecru through the pasta maker, using setting #1, #3, and finally #5. This makes it a lot easier to run through the pasta machine. Cut two ⁵⁄₈" by ⁵⁄₈" squares. Press one square around each ear of corn. It won't quite fit. Have the bottom of the squares line up and curl the top of each square. Press the two ears of corn together slightly. Bake and set aside.

Man

1. Legs. Roll a ⅞" ball of gray into a 3" long log. Bend the log in half, and press the halves together.

2. Shoes. Roll two ⅜" balls of black into ½" long logs. Flatten the logs into ovals, and press them to the legs.

3. Body. Roll a ⅞" ball of gray into a 1¼" long cone. Set the cone on top of the legs, and gently press down. Press a wire halfway into the top of the body to stabilize the head.

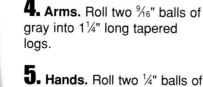

4. Arms. Roll two ⁹⁄₁₆" balls of gray into 1¼" long tapered logs.

5. Hands. Roll two ¼" balls of beige into teardrops. Flatten the teardrops and press them to the widest end of the arms. Press the arms to the top of the body. Make sure the tops of the arms are even with the top of the body. Curl the arms around.

6. Collar. Gradually flatten a sheet of white through the pasta maker, using setting #1, #3, and finally #5. This makes it a lot easier to run through the pasta machine. Use a knife to cut a ⁵⁄₈" by ¾" rectangle. Press the collar to the top of the body.

7. Bow. Using part of the black sheet from Step 6, cut a ¹⁄₁₆" by 1" strip. Fold each end to the middle. Roll a ¹⁄₁₆" ball of black, and press it on the center of the bow. Roll two ¹⁄₁₆" balls of black into ⁵⁄₁₆" long tapered logs. Place the logs on the collar, and then press the bow onto the collar, covering the top of the logs.

8. Place the pumpkin into the man's hands.

9. Head. Roll a ¹³⁄₁₆" ball of beige.

10. Eyes. Press two seed beads into the head. Use a toothpick to make two squint lines by each eye.

11. Use a cotton swab to apply blush to the cheeks.

12. Hair. Roll two ⁵⁄₁₆" balls of raw sienna into teardrops. Flatten the teardrops, allow the tails to cross over each other, and press them to the head.

13. Ears. Roll two ⅛" balls of beige. Flatten them slightly, and press them onto each side of the head. Make two lines in each ear.

14. Press the head to the top of the body.

15. Hat. Roll a ⁹⁄₁₆" ball of gray, and flatten it to a 1⅛" circle to create the rim. Press the rim to the top of the head. Roll a ⁹⁄₁₆" ball of gray and flatten it into a trapezoid. Press the trapezoid to the top of the rim. Gradually flatten a sheet of black through the pasta maker, using setting #1, #3, and finally #5. Use your knife to cut a ⅛" wide strip. Press the strip around the base of the hat and cut off the excess where the ends meet.

16. Buckle. Roll a ³⁄₃₂" ball of gold into a ¾" long log. Shape the log into a square. I do that by pinching the clay to make the corners. Press it to the front of the hat.

Woman

1. Body. Roll a 1" ball of gray into a cone. Insert the blunt end of a paintbrush half way into the cone. Gently roll the paintbrush back and forth to thin out the cone. Reposition the paintbrush, and continue until the body is about ⅛" thick on the lower half of the cone.

2. Legs. Roll two ⁷⁄₁₆" balls of white into 1" long tapered logs.

3. Shoes. Roll two ¼" balls of black, and flatten them into ovals. Press the shoes to the wider end of the legs. Press the narrow ends of the legs together, and press them to the body.

4. Arms and Hands. Create as for the Man (steps 4 and 5).

5. Collar and Bow. Create as for the Man (steps 6 and 7).

6. Press the corn into the woman's hands.

7. Head. Create as for the Man (step 9).

8. Eyes. Create as for the Man (step 10).

9. Use a cotton swab to apply blush to the cheeks.

10. Hair. Flatten a sheet of raw sienna to a #3 setting on the pasta maker. Cut two ¾" by 1" rectangles. Curl the end of each strip, and press one onto each side of the head.

11. Cut a ¾" triangle, curl the end, and trim it to fit the opening in the back, left by the first two strips.

12. Hat. Cut a ¾" by 1¾" triangle from the sheet of white clay used to create the Man's collar (step 6). Gently bend the triangle in half, and pinch the center fold. Open the ends, place the hat on the woman's head, and curl the front ends.

13. Press the head to the body.

Ginger and Fred Christmas Ornaments

Cookie cutters are a great foundation for polymer clay projects. They come in a wide range of shapes and sizes. It's just like decorating Christmas cookies. These will look great on your Christmas tree. You can also glue a magnet on the back and use them on your refrigerator. Remember not to use cookie cutters for food after using them for clay.

materials

- Premo! Sculpey: raw sienna (2 blocks), white, cadmium red, green, and black
  pink—mix a $\frac{3}{8}$" ball of white with a $\frac{1}{8}$" ball of red
- 2 eye pins
- Toothpick
- $\frac{7}{16}$" Kemper circle cutter
- $\frac{3}{16}$" Kemper heart cutter
- 3" gingerbread man and woman cookie cutters
- Pasta maker or acrylic brayer

1. Body. Roll a sheet of raw sienna through the pasta maker at a #1 setting. Use the cookie cutters to cut out a gingerbread man and woman.

2. Make a candy cane log (see page 10), and outline each body with the log.

3. Eyes. Roll two $\frac{3}{32}$" balls of white into teardrops, and flatten the teardrops. Press the narrow ends together, and press them to the face. For pupils, roll two $\frac{1}{32}$" balls of black, and press one onto each eye.

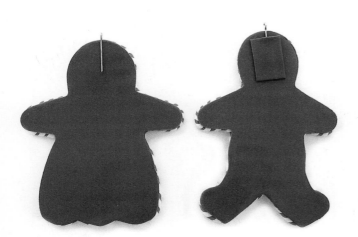

4. **Eyebrows.** Roll two ⅛" balls of raw sienna into tapered logs, and press one around the top of each eye.

5. **Nose.** Roll a ³⁄₁₆" ball of raw sienna, and press it below the eyes.

6. **Mouth.** Use the circle cutter to make the mouth.

7. **Hearts.** Gradually flatten a sheet of pink through the pasta maker, using setting #1, #3, and finally #5. This makes it a lot easier to run through the pasta machine. Use the heart cutter to cut out two hearts, and press one at each end of the mouth.

8. **Buttons.** Roll three ⅛" balls of green, and press them to the body. Use the blunt end of a paintbrush to indent the center of each button. Use a toothpick to make two buttonholes.

9. Gradually flatten a sheet of raw sienna through the pasta maker, using setting #1, #3, and finally #5. Cut a ¾" by ½" rectangle. Press the eye pin to the back of the figure. Press a piece of clay over the eye pin.

Resources

American Art Clay Company (AMACO)
4717 W. 16th Street
Indianapolis, IN 46222
(800) 374-1600
www.amaco.com
Distributor of FIMO and FIMO Soft, push molds, books, and videos

Blumenhaus Florist
(651) 387-8550

Clay Factory of Escondido
P.O. Box 460598
Escondido, CA 92046-0598
(877) 728-5739
www.clayfactoryinc.com
Distributor of Premo! Sculpey, Sculpey III, Amazing Eraser Clay, Granitex, and texture plates

Krause Publications
700 E. State Street
Iola, WI 54990
(800) 258-0929
www.krause.com
Publisher of magazines and books

Becky Meverden
becky@meverden.net
www.meverden.net

Off The Beaten Path
6601 D. Royal Street
Pleasant Valley, MO 64068
(816) 415-8827
www.cookiecutter.com
Cookie cutters in all shapes and sizes

Polyform Products
1601 Estes Avenue
Elk Grove Village, IL 60007
(847) 427-0020
www.sculpey.com
Manufacturer of Amazing Eraser Clay, Granitex, Premo! Sculpey, Sculpey III, activity sets, polymer clay accessories, and the EZ Release Push Molds

Prairie Craft Company
P.O. Box 209
Florissant, CO 80816-0209
(800) 779-0615
www.prairiecraft.com
Distributor of Kato Polyclay, Kato polymer clay tools, polymer clay videos, Kemper tools, and Atlas pasta makers

Toner Plastics
699 Silver Street
Agawam, MA 01001
(413) 789-1300
www.tonerplastics.com
Distributor for Fun Wire

Wee Folk Creations
18476 Natchez Avenue
Prior Lake, MN 55372
(888) 933-3655
www.weefolk.com
Distributor of FIMO products, Sculpey products, videos, books, Kemper tools, texture plates, and other assorted polymer clay tools